Flip the Flaps
Planet Earth

Dr Mike Goldsmith and Nicki Palin

KINGFISHER

KINGFISHER

First published 2010 by Kingfisher
an imprint of Macmillan Children's Books
a division of Macmillan Publishers Limited
20 New Wharf Road, London N1 9RR
Basingstoke and Oxford
Associated companies throughout the world
www.panmacmillan.com

Consultant: Professor Robert Francis

ISBN 978-0-7534-1739-3

1 3 5 7 9 8 6 4 2
1TR/1109/TOPLF/UNTD/140MA/C

A CIP catalogue record for this book is available from the British Library.

Printed in China

Contents

Planet Earth

The Earth is where we live, a planet that spins through space. If you flew to the Moon in a rocket, you would see the Earth in the sky, like a huge, bright disc coloured blue and white.

night

day

Earth

Sun

4

1. A planet is a huge ball of rock or gas that moves around the Sun.

2. Yes. The Earth spins round once a day.

3. At night, the Sun shines on the other side of the Earth. So it is day there when it is night where you are.

The path of the Earth

It takes a year for the Earth to go once around the Sun.

After six months, the Earth has gone half-way round.

Air

The air is all around us.
We need air to breathe.
Clouds float in it, birds
fly in it, and we call it
wind when it moves.

people climbing

6

1. Air is a mixture of gases. Oxygen is one of these gases, which we need to breathe.

2. The atmosphere is the layer of air that covers the Earth like a blanket.

3. No. The atmosphere fades away the higher up it goes. There is no air at all a few kilometres above the Earth.

People climbing high mountains take air with them to breathe.

The atmosphere

satellite – 1,000 kilometres up

shooting stars – 100 kilometres up

jumbo jet – 10 kilometres up

7

Life on Earth

Planet Earth is full of life because there is air and water here. Fish swim in the oceans, birds swoop through the air, and many other animals run on the ground, or burrow beneath it.

panda

young bamboo shoots

bird

8

butterfly

1. Yes. There are things living in the deepest oceans, the highest mountains, and even the hottest and coldest places on Earth.

2. Yes. Plants live and grow – and they breathe, too!

3. The blue whale is the largest animal on Earth. It's as heavy as 2,500 people!

There are many types of life on Earth.

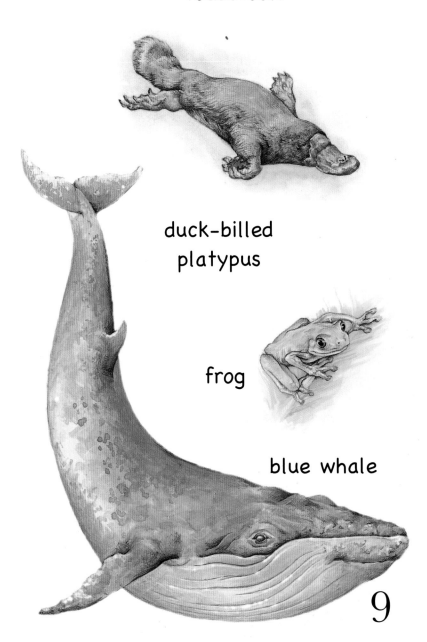

toadstools

duck-billed platypus

frog

blue whale

9

The oceans

Most of Earth is covered in blue oceans of salty water, full of fish and other living things. In some places, the water is frozen into shining white ice.

boat

puffins

seal

10

turtle

1. There are five oceans.
They are called the Arctic,
Atlantic, Indian, Pacific
and Southern oceans.

2. The ocean has a floor,
with mountains and valleys.

squid

3. Waves are made by winds,
blowing across the ocean.

deep-sea
anglerfish

11

Inside our planet

If you dug a hole under your house, you might find many things: soil or concrete... even tunnels or caves! But under this, inside the Earth, you would soon reach a thick layer of solid rock.

one side of the Earth

1. No. The deeper you go underground, the hotter it gets.

2. Deep underground it is so hot that the rocks melt and become liquid.

3. There is a huge ball of metal, called the core, in the middle of the Earth.

Inside Earth's surface layer

plant roots and a water pipe

ancient ruins

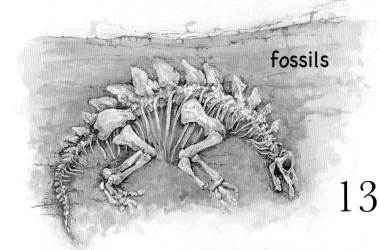

fossils

13

Earthquakes

Sometimes the earth shakes and trembles, and huge cracks may appear in the ground. Buildings crack and crumble, and some fall down. This is an earthquake.

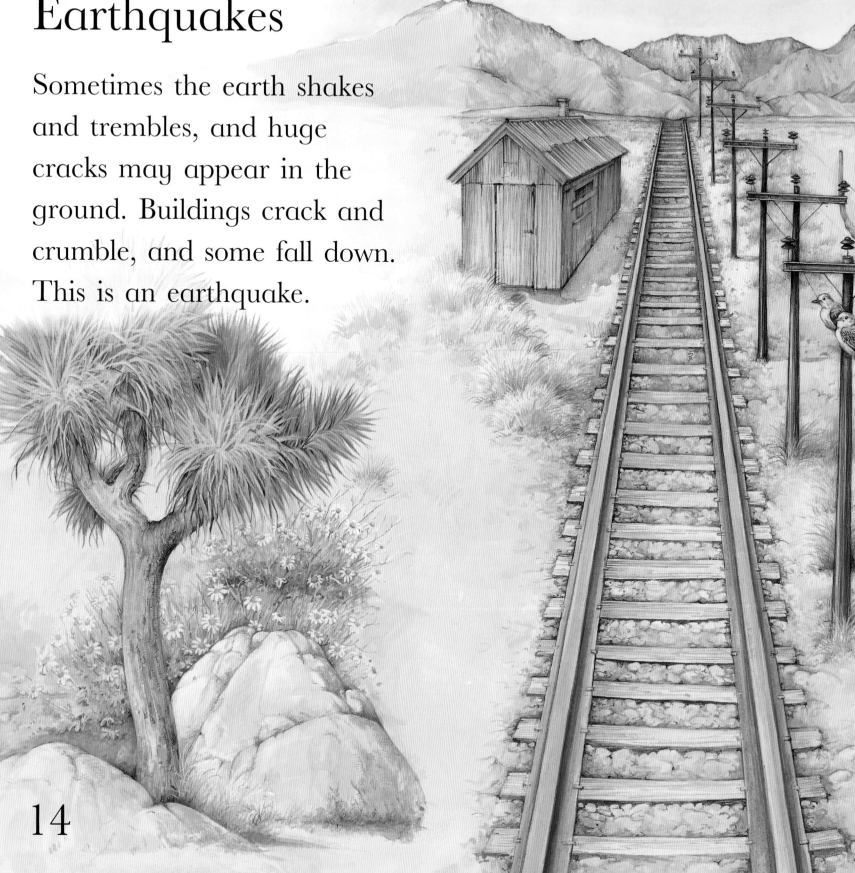

14

1. Deep underground, huge pieces of rock scrape slowly past each other. Sometimes, they slip suddenly, making the land above them shake.

2. 'Quake' is another word for 'shake'.

3. No, but we can make buildings that do not fall down when an earthquake happens.

Why the ground shakes

Most of the time, the rocky plates below Earth's surface move slowly...

...but sometimes, they suddenly slip.

Volcanoes

Not all mountains are quiet and still. Some of them can throw out smoke and fire, like huge fireworks! Mountains like this are called volcanoes.

1. Lava is very hot liquid rock from deep inside the Earth. It sometimes flows out of volcanoes.

An island is formed

underwater volcano erupts

volcano grows larger

2. No. Volcanoes are found only in some parts of the world.

volcano cools and plants appear

3. Yes. Sometimes the lava from these volcanoes turns into new islands.

a new island has formed

17

Index